OUR WORLD NATIONAL GEOGRAPHIC

Hare Is Scared

A Folktale from Africa
Retold by Elizabeth Emende

NATIONAL GEOGRAPHIC LEARNING | CENGAGE Learning

Listen children.
This is a story about
Hare and his friends,
Monkey and Elephant.

2

One day, Hare is walking to his house.
He does not know it, but there is
something inside his house!

"Don't come in!" says the thing in Hare's house.
"I like to eat hares!"

Is it a monster? Hare is scared.

4

Hare sees Monkey. Hare says, "There is a monster in my house!" Now Hare is crying.

"I can help you," says Monkey.

Monkey goes to Hare's door.

"Don't come in!" says the monster. "I'm very hungry. I like to eat monkeys, too!"

Now Monkey and Hare are really scared! Who can help them?

Hare and Monkey go to Elephant.

"Of course, I can help you!" says Elephant.
"I am big. I'm not scared of a monster!"

Elephant goes to Hare's house.

"Don't come in!" says the monster.

"I am very big!" says Elephant. "You can't eat me!"

Mouse comes out.

"A mouse!" cries Elephant. "Eeek!"
Now Elephant is scared. He runs away!

"Are you angry with me?" Now Hare and Monkey are laughing.

"No! We're happy," says Hare. "You made us laugh!"

11

Facts About Animals

Pets have special ways to show their feelings. Look at how these two cats show their feelings.

It puts its ears down.

It puts its back up.

It puffs out the fur on its tail.

It makes hissing sounds.

This cat is scared.

It puts its tail up.

It has a straight back.

It puts its ears up.

This cat is happy.

Fun with Feelings

Write the word for each picture.

angry   happy   sad   scared

angry

Write the letters to make the words.

laughing
sad
crying
angry
happy

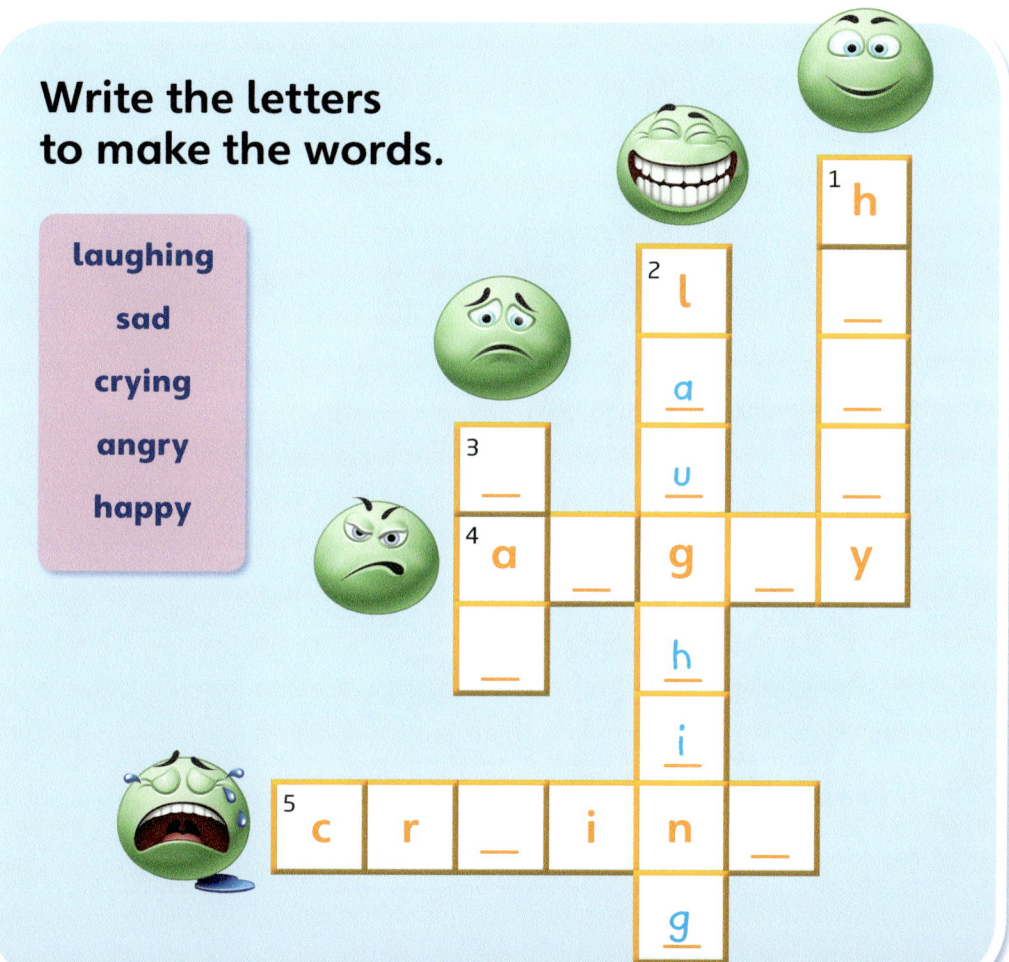

Glossary

hare

elephant

monkey

monster

mouse